The Heart of Grief Relief

JOURNAL

The path to grief relief is through the heart.

RICHARD BALLO

Praise for *The Heart of Grief Relief Journal*

"Richard Ballo provides a long-needed and powerfully therapeutic tool created not only to ease one's grief, but in addition, to allow the reader to actively participate in the process of re-contextualizing his or her loss. *The Heart of Grief Relief Journal* provides the difficult answers to the questions that exist at the very core of the human experience."

–David Perlmutter, M.D., FACN
Author of the #1 *New York Times* Best Seller *Grain Brain*, star of the PBS special *BrainChange* and one of four of Dr. Oz's "go to" physicians in the U.S.A.

"Richard Ballo's *The Heart of Grief Relief Journal* is a book for real life–a life full of loves and full of losses that sometimes cause profound grief. Many years ago I lost a love… When I open this journal, the words of those who know my grief, like Rich Ballo, speak to me. Let them speak to you. From their words…form your words…speak your grief, your memories, your despair and your love. And most hopefully, this journal will help you, speak your peace."

–Karen Rollins
Hospice President and CEO, Avow, Naples, Florida

"Having many years of funeral service as a funeral director and owner, I can directly comprehend the need and value of a grieving person to journal their thoughts and feelings. This expression can facilitate the grieving process where one can begin to believe in their new journey."

–Juliana Berring Fuller
Former owner and funeral director, Fuller Funeral Homes

"When a friend suffers a death in the family, one often doesn't quite know what to do for them. Rich Ballo's new book is more than a journal; it is replete with practical ideas to cope with death of a loved one, drawn from his own grief experience. These include 'hospice for the living' and concrete ways to cope with holidays. This book would make a gentle gift for a survivor on their grief journey."

–Diana Jacks, Ph.D.
Author of the award-winning book, *Here to There, Grief to Peace*

"As a fellow sojourner on the path of grief, Rich Ballo invites those on their journey to walk with him as he provides encouragement, hope, support and some helpful ways to begin 'getting it all out' with *The Heart of Grief Relief Journal*. Writing from the soul helped Rich get to the heart of his grief, and I believe this wonderful guide will help others do the same."

–Larry Dawalt, Masters of Divinity
Senior Director of Spiritual & Grief Care Services
Hospice & Palliative Care Charlotte (NC) Region

"I wish I had read Rich's journal when my 54-year-old husband died a few years ago after being sick for only two months. In this book Rich offers a bounty of beautiful quotes to help lift the heaviness of any grieving heart. His words of advice will ring true, regardless of the type of loss someone has experienced. *The Heart of Grief Relief Journal* brings hope, just when it is needed most, validating that grief is a process, not an event. I recommend it for anyone who is bereaved and believe it to be an important resource for grief support groups in hospices, churches, and other organizations."

–Karla Wheeler–Founder and President of Quality of Life Publishing Co.
Publishers of numerous award-winning grief support books

"Rich Ballo's *The Heart of Grief Relief Kit* is a truly comprehensive and practical resource for those who have lost a loved one, their family and friends and for grief care professionals also. The kit offers a unique variety of helpful strategies, such as storytelling and journaling, plus encouraging quotes and other useful materials. Through heartfelt personal experiences and meaningful reflections, the author offers an array of realistic and self-affirming ideas to help us move along our grief journey on a path to peace and healing."

> **–Cricket Weston**
> Retired Director of Communications & Education—Hospice & Palliative Care
> Charlotte (NC) Region

"It is reassuring to read the words of someone else who understands first-hand about grief. Rich's time-tested tips for handling holidays and special occasions will be especially useful to folks newly bereaved. Like Rich, my husband discovered coping-group work with others recently bereaved to be especially meaningful and supportive. I also found journaling helpful after our children were killed in separate automobile accidents. We feel this journal and kit have something to help everyone."

> **–Wendy & Rob Lindsay**
> Their story regarding the death of both their son and daughter is featured in
> *Afterglow: Signs of Continued Love*

"I think Rich Ballo's *The Heart of Grief Relief Journal* will help anyone who has experienced a loss, especially grieving teens. After my dad died when I was 14, I found that talking with my mom and a few close friends helped me work through my grief. But sometimes, my feelings couldn't easily be expressed in conversations with others, so journaling became a safe place for me to not only write down words, but also to draw pictures as a healthy outlet for my sometimes overwhelming emotions."

> **–Jenny Lee Wheeler**
> Author of the national award-winning book, *Weird Is Normal When Teenagers Grieve*

"For anyone in grief who has ever tried to keep a journal, Rich Ballo's *The Heart of Grief Relief Journal* is a must-read book. His clear and valuable suggestions offer readers truly practical ways to approach their vulnerability in a safe and comforting way. And the many inspirational quotes are wonderful 'prompts' or starting points for processing grief in productive ways. I highly recommend this book to anyone in that first, very difficult year who feels lost in the midst of loss and seeks ways of surviving— and thriving—in the days ahead."

> **–Jeanette Leardi, M.A.**
> Instructor of journaling, storytelling, personal myth-making, and memoir-writing as
> therapeutic tools for healing

The Heart of Grief Relief Journal

Published and Distributed by
Tolman Main Press
5430 Jaeger Road, Suite #102, Naples, FL 34109

Copyright 2015 by Richard Ballo

All rights reserved.

The Heart of Grief Relief Journal and *Life without Lisa* are available at special quantity discounts for bulk purchase for sales promotions, premiums, fund-raising and educational needs. Special books or book excerpts also can be created to fit specific needs.

For details, write Tolman Main Press
5430 Jaeger Road, Suite #102, Naples, FL 34109
www.tolmanmainpress.com

ISBN 978-0-9885469-0-5

Editorial services: Jill H. Lawrence, Ruby Slippers, Inc.
Book interior and cover: Dave Aldrich, www.aldrichdesign.com

Printed in the U.S.A.

Visit us at www.TheHeartofGriefRelief.com, www.TolmanMainPress.com or www.RichardBallo.com

DEDICATION

*The Heart of Grief Relief Journal and its kit are dedicated to
Avow of Naples, Florida. The wonderful, loving, committed people
who make up Avow are doing such meaningful work.
They not only provide relief and support to those who are making
their transition back into spirit, but also are playing a major role
in assisting the families of those who have suffered the loss of their
loved one. It's impossible to give enough credit and to express
sufficient gratitude and respect to these devoted people.*

ALSO BY RICHARD BALLO:

*Life without Lisa—A Widowed Father's
Compelling Journey Through the Rough Seas of Grief*

The Heart of Grief Relief Kit
Please see pages 207-208 for a description of the kit components and how to order.

ACKNOWLEDGEMENTS

THERE ARE MANY PEOPLE TO THANK for their help bringing this journal to life in order to help those dealing with grief.

I would like to thank Jill Lawrence of Ruby Slippers, Inc. for her creativity, ingenuity and tireless work behind the scenes to bring this project to life. Thanks to Debbie Darling for proofreading, and Dave Aldrich of Aldrich Design for his great cover design and interior layout.

The authors and thinkers whose quotes spoke to the heart of grief that I used on the pages of this journal also deserve acknowledgement. Often such words of wisdom and inspiration help take us through the darkest of times. I am grateful to be able to provide a platform to share their words with many who may be bolstered by them.

I would like to thank Avow for their outstanding community service as well as for giving me the opportunity as a volunteer to assist in spreading the word of the hospice mission and, as a result, meeting so many great people. I would also like to thank the doctors, social workers, and authors who believed in this project and gave me support and encouragement.

To my sons Victor and Nick and Victor's children, my grandkids, Nolan and Leland, who bring joy to my life and help me keep life in perspective.

My heartfelt gratitude goes to all.

Rich Ballo

Rich Ballo

CONTENTS

Write about Your Grief in Order to Heal

ANYONE WHO HAS LOST A BELOVED to death knows all too well the challenges involved in facing the reality and finality of that death. Inexplicably the loss is compounded when guilt, depression, and despair often overwhelm those left behind. Grief takes on tsunami proportions with the seeming power to devastate a life–at least that's how it feels when grief is new and beyond measure. What can you do to weather the storm? You can either tie yourself to a tree to brace for the impact like islanders have been known to do in order to survive a tsunami or run as fast as you can in the other direction in an attempt to evade and escape.

Will it be the tree and rope approach or running for your life? Confront or repress? The odds of outrunning a tsunami are slim to none, but grief can be repressed over the short term. Be assured that repression will not get you where you want to go since it only sublimates grief, it most definitely does not eliminate it. Like a beach ball being held under water, it will eventually pop back up to give us an opportunity to confront it and work through it. Like it or not, confronting and dealing with grief provides the way to live again. So grab a rope, pick out a worthy tree and brace for the impact.

Give voice to your grief

When death does invade your life, the very best advice one can follow is to give grief expression, acknowledgement and go through the often-painful recovery process–a literary-licensed version of tree lashing. Grief cannot and should not be denied. Fully confronting grief is critical if you want to heal after suffering a loss. Tamping down, denying grief and running from it only delays the healing process. Failing to talk about it and express your heartfelt feelings only postpone the inevitable and increase the depth and duration of suffering.

Recognizing your own deep feelings and allowing your grief to be expressed will make all the difference in the world. Share with a trusted friend and keep a journal of your thoughts and feelings. Seek help from a professional if you aren't making progress. Working with a Hospice counselor or grief therapist can be tremendously beneficial.

Being able to talk and write about what you are going through and how you feel will yield positive results. Even though it seems impossible, expressing grief brings acceptance, healing and charts the course for your living a happy life again. You will amazingly survive the onslaught and be able to untie yourself from the tree to go forward to forge a new life.

This journal is your lifeline–hang onto it

This journal is dedicated to your process. Use it daily to give words to your deepest feelings, anguish, hopes and seemingly impossible dreams. Confront and face the tsunami head on. You will survive. Generously give yourself time to heal and allow for the seemingly improbable promise of a new, happy tomorrow.

Fill these pages. Embrace the process. Expect a miraculous healing. Look toward a new tomorrow.

Introduction to Richard Ballo's
The Heart of Grief Relief Journal

THE SECOND OUR LOVED ONE DIES and leaves this earth, the lives of those who either loved the deceased or had a significant relationship with the deceased, will change. The depth of that change and breadth of the grief is deeply personal and individual. Some individuals will take a long fall into the land of grief, the shadow-land far below the surface of day-to-day life. These individuals will likely find themselves walking in two worlds, each eerily unfamiliar. Most grapple with how best to cope.

One of the more profoundly helpful coping mechanisms is journaling. It is a tool that assists in documenting, memorializing, remembering and navigating the way through this dark passage. It is also an effective tool for helping to integrate the experience of profound loss and ultimately integrating the two worlds. Journaling can be a tool that helps reassemble our shattered aspects to make us whole again.

The reflective nature of grief combined with the act of journaling in the present moment slowly bring these two worlds back together. When we take the time to reflect on our lives, our memories, our secret treasures, our joyful moments, as well as our deepest regrets, healing becomes possible. All of these elements make up the experiences which likely continue to influence who we are. Relationships, whether they are rich with love or fraught with pain and struggle shape us. Journaling helps us to see how significant people in our lives have impacted us, our body, mind and spirit. Ultimately journaling may grant us the empowerment to actively participate in determining who we will become as a result of having been touched by those who once walked this earth with us.

The author of this unique grief journal, Richard Ballo, is a colleague and friend. I know how much journaling helped him heal after he lost his wife. Both he and I most sincerely hope you enjoy the same benefits.

Rich was only 39 when he suffered the loss of his beloved 38-year-old wife Lisa to cancer. He was engulfed in a grief so deep that he could barely get out of bed. But once he began to journal his feelings and thoughts, his life gradually took a more positive turn.

It turns out Rich intuitively knew that journaling would be best for him. He later discovered the significant amount of scientific research that proves journaling strengthens the immune system thereby counteracting the negative impact emotional stress has on a body. Scientists have proven that journaling improves cognitive function which means you can think more clearly. Clear thinking is often blurred by grief.

Research has repeatedly validated that journaling can reduce the symptoms of asthma and arthritis as well as other health challenges so it can benefit your wellbeing in specific ways. By journaling, you'll enjoy decreased levels of stress, be better able to cope with trauma including emotional trauma, and experience less worry and anxiety —a veritable treasure-trove of benefits from the simple act of writing your thoughts and feelings.

Rich recommends writing your deepest feelings coupled with thoughts about losing your loved one. A study published in the *Annals of Behavioral Medicine* showed that people who wrote about a traumatic event gained the most benefit when they included both thoughts and feelings rather than merely writing about emotions alone.

In order to heal, your grief needs to be expressed in a safe way. A journal is incredibly safe. The pages of a journal are non-judgmental, never get bored with what you write and will always be there for you. The pages want your words, your deepest, even darkest thoughts because those of us who grieve often harbor such thoughts.

This *The Heart of Grief Relief Journal* is from the heart of a man who knows grief intimately and has recovered thanks in major part to the journaling process. Rich also recommends joining a hospice support group, taking advantage of hospice one-on-one counseling, letting yourself cry and admitting where you are in the healing process. Healing from grief is not necessarily easy, but neither is building a house —a truism Rich often points out. Yet both can be accomplished in stages as long as you start with a solid foundation. Journaling is one of the best tools you can use to build your foundation.

Please remember that the path to grief relief is through the heart–I wish you a meaningful, healing heart-centered journaling journey.

Louise Kenny, LCSW
Bereavement Services Coordinator,
Avow Hospice, Naples, Florida
Dorland Health Silver Crown Award winner
for excellence in providing senior services

The Heart of Grief Relief

JOURNAL

The path to grief relief is through the heart.

RICHARD BALLO

Men and women alike benefit from putting words on paper:

Journaling Paves the Way for Healing in the Wake of Life's Greatest Traumas

COMEDIAN AND GOLDEN GLOBE WINNER Tim Allen, *Toy Story* and *Wild Hogs* star not to mention TV star of *Home Improvement* and *Last Man Standing*, shot to fame and fortune by grunting. We all laughed as Tim expressed his heartfelt feelings through a grunt here and a series of grunts there. Why did it make us laugh? Because, like all comedy that really hits home, it was based on the truth that most men have a tough time expressing feelings.

But keeping everything bottled up inside is not considered to be a psychologically healthy behavior according to experts. Yet when push comes to shove, most men, when confronted by life's deepest feelings and issues, clam up and often rely on grunts or their equivalent to cloak what they're feeling.

Although women generally express their feelings more readily than men, there are times when they also bottle up their feelings because the pain is seemingly just too intense to confront or they soldier-up for the sake of appearing to be strong for others, especially for their children. This repression approach is equally destructive for both men and women.

Putting words on paper saved me

I was no different from any other man in that regard, but my saving grace was my ability and desire to write my feelings and experiences down on paper. So when disaster struck and my beloved 38-year-old wife, Lisa, died of cancer, I committed my overwhelming feelings to my journal. Paper captured my anguish and tears, my darkest thoughts and hopelessness. I believe having this escape valve for my devastating emotions probably saved me, along with my love for Victor and Nick who were only six and five when their mother died in 1993.

A year before Lisa's death, we decided to make a major change in climate and geography. We decided to leave Massachusetts. We bought and furnished a home in Naples, Florida. I shipped my clothes and my car to Naples. We registered the kids for school in Collier County. We readied our Massachusetts house for our absence. But our "best laid plans" never came to total fruition.

On a trip back to Massachusetts Lisa entered the hospital and two months later she died. She would not fulfill her dream of living in Florida.

1

Lisa's decidedly premature death was a shock to everyone except her closest nursing friends. Although she had been diagnosed with cancer nearly four years prior, both she and I firmly believed she was beating it. But in the end, Lisa succumbed to the disease leaving our little boys and me reeling from the loss and crippled by intolerable grief.

I freely admit, after Lisa died I had no desire to continue living and had it not been for my two sons who needed me so desperately, I would have made no attempt to resume normal life. I could not fathom ever smiling again or feeling any small bit of happiness from being alive, let alone being exhilarated and excited about life. From my point of view, I was as good as dead. Everything inside me died along with Lisa.

I walked around the Massachusetts house not knowing what to do with myself. My life was in limbo. I was in Massachusetts yet we had been in Florida. My car, my clothes, and my mind were in Florida.

I loyally followed the plan we had mapped out together

The only clear picture that kept coming into my mind time and time again was our new life and house in Naples. So on a bright and cold January day, the boys and I left Massachusetts for our home in Florida just as we had done many times over the past year. But my heart wasn't in it this time. My heart really wasn't in anything because Lisa wasn't with us.

Once we got settled in Naples, I went to the local Hospice and enrolled both the boys and me in appropriate support groups. I was pleased to discover that Avow Hospice offered a children's support group at the local elementary school. That was ideal. As far as my support group was concerned, I found the process to be exceedingly painful at first, but eventually lifesaving. The boys thoroughly enjoyed their Hospice experience and were relieved to learn that other children had also lost parents, and they were not alone.

It took years before I felt some sense of hope and happiness again. But in the dark days I recorded all my ups and downs, highs and lows in my journal. My motive was to remember what had happened and keeping a journal was a safe and natural place for me to pour out the truth from my painful perspective. As a result, it was a frank and honest record of my own journey from unthinkable loss to recovery. It certainly was not written for publication. Nonetheless, my journal became a published book as a result of my meeting Karla Wheeler, a fellow parent at my sons' school. Karla, Founder and President of Quality of Life Publishing, established a publishing company that focuses on end-of-life, grief and hospice related issues.

My grief journal is transformed into a book

Karla and I naturally talked about my grief journey, and I told her I had recorded my entire process in my journal. She asked me to share with her what I had written. Karla immediately saw healing value for others in my words.

"I knew Rich's experience, because he told his story so frankly and honestly, could help others who had lost their spouses, especially men," Karla remembers. "I knew this could give others much needed hope."

The result was the award-winning book, *Life without Lisa—A Widowed Father's Compelling Journey Through the Rough Seas of Grief.* It chronicles my personal, heart-wrenching progression from truly believing my life was not worth living to a triumphant, happy return to a fully vibrant life.

My life is not the same as it was before Lisa died, of course. But it, nonetheless, is wonderful in a different way. I've grown, evolved and so have the boys. I never would have believed that to be possible which is why I want to hold out hope for everyone who has suffered a devastating loss.

No matter how impossible it is to believe, life can be beautiful again. My sons and I are living proof. I can smile again with the assurance of a man who has been there, done that.

Rich Ballo

"When our heart is broken,
it is also wide open."

~ John Welshons, *Awakening from Grief*

_____

_____

_____

_____

_____

_____

_____

_____

_____

_____

_____

_____

_____

_____

_____

_____

_____

_____

_____

_____

_____

_____

_____

_____

_____

_____

_____

_____

_____

_____

"There are others walking this path
this very moment. You are not alone…"
~ Diana Jacks, *Here to There, Grief to Peace*

"As I fought my way from overwhelming grief to the renewing Light, I discovered reading books of a spiritual nature brought me some measure of comfort. It was my first step on a very long road to learning how to cope with my devastating loss."

~ Sandy Wiltshire, *My Gift of Light*

_____

_____

_____

_____

_____

_____

_____

_____

_____

_____

_____

_____

_____

_____

_____

"Life is eternal, and love is immortal;
and death is only a horizon; and a horizon
is nothing save the limit of our sight."
~ Rossiter Worthington Raymond 1840-1918

"Give sorrow words. The grief that does not speak
whispers the o'erfraught heart and bids it break."

~ William Shakespeare, *Macbeth*

_____

_____

_____

_____

_____

_____

_____

_____

_____

_____

_____

_____

_____

_____

_____

_____

_____

_____

_____

_____

_____

_____

_____

_____

_____

_____

_____

_____

_____

"The process of opening our hearts to all of it is the process of healing grief."

~ John E. Welshons, *Awakening from Grief*

"Do not stand at my grave and weep,
I am not there; I do not sleep.
I am a thousand winds that blow,
I am the diamond glints on snow,
I am the sunlight on ripened grain,
I am the gentle autumn rain.
When you awaken in the morning's hush
I am the swift uplifting rush
Of quiet birds in circled flight.
I am the soft stars that shine at night.
Do not stand at my grave and cry,
I am not there; I did not die."

~ Mary Elizabeth Frye 1932

_____

_____

_____

_____

_____

_____

_____

_____

_____

_____

_____

_____

_____

_____

_____

_____

_____

"Honest listening is one of the best medicines
we can offer the dying and the bereaved."
~ Jean Cameron

"When I didn't know how I would handle (grief)
another moment, I left the house and walked."

~ Sandy Wiltshire, *My Gift of Light*

_____

_____

_____

_____

_____

_____

_____

_____

_____

_____

_____

_____

_____

_____

_____

_____

"A friend is someone who reaches for
your hand, but touches your heart."
~ Author unknown

"I want to heal my heart and live again. I owe it to myself and the kids… . Right now I have to let the tears and the pain flow out...the grief counselor (told) me it was okay–even good–to cry."

~ Richard Ballo, *Life without Lisa*

_____

_____

_____

_____

_____

_____

_____

_____

_____

_____

_____

_____

_____

_____

_____

_____

_____

_____

_____

"Argue for your limitations
and sure enough, they're yours."
~ Richard Bach, *Illusions*

"To me, I died. I saw the place where you go when you die.
I am not afraid of dying. What I learned there is that the most
important thing is loving while you are alive."
11-year-old boy Jason reporting his near death experience.
~ Dr. Raymond Moody, M.D., Ph.D., *The Light Beyond*

_____

_____

_____

_____

_____

_____

_____

_____

_____

_____

_____

_____

_____

_____

_____

_____

_____

_____

_____

_____

_____

_____

_____

_____

_____

_____

_____

_____

"The deepest grief of all is the death of a loved one. For many, that grief is greatly relieved by accounts of near-death experiences."
~ Dr. Raymond Moody, M.D., Ph.D., *The Light Beyond*

"Mourn not for those that live, nor those that die....
Never the spirit was born; the spirit shall
cease to be never..."

~ Bhagavad-Gita

_____

_____

_____

_____

_____

_____

_____

_____

_____

_____

_____

_____

_____

_____

"Peace I leave with you, my peace I give
unto you; not as the world giveth, give I
unto you. Let not your heart be troubled,
neither let it be afraid."
~ The Holy Bible, John 14:27

"Activities like writing (keeping a journal of your feelings, writing poems or letters to your loved one), art…music…and other healthy activities that come naturally to you are also good ways to express some of the emotions you are feeling."

~ Jenny Wheeler, *Weird Is Normal When Teenagers Grieve*

_____

_____

_____

_____

_____

_____

_____

_____

_____

_____

_____

_____

_____

_____

"Death leaves a heartache no one can heal,
love leaves a memory no one can steal."

~ from a headstone in Ireland

"Sorrow makes us all children again—destroys all differences of intellect. The wisest know nothing."

~ Ralph Waldo Emerson

_____

_____

_____

_____

_____

_____

_____

_____

_____

_____

_____

_____

_____

_____

_____

_____

"The voice of Nature loudly cries
And many a message from the skies,
That something in us never dies."
~ Robert Burns

"You did not die.

You live in the beautiful wind that blows

You live in the sound of birds that crow

You live in the sun that shines so bright

You live in the peaceful dark at night

You live in a star I see in the sky

You live in the ocean waves that come in with the tide

You live in the smell of flowers and grass

You live in the summer that goes so fast

You live in my heart that hurts so much

You did not die, we only lost touch."

Written by 16-year-old Shari after her brother's death
Published in *Good Grief–Healing Through the Shadow of Loss*

_____

_____

_____

_____

_____

_____

_____

_____

_____

_____

_____

_____

_____

_____

"The risk of love is loss, and the price of loss is grief. But the pain of grief is only a shadow when compared with the pain of never risking love."

~ Hilary Stanton Zunin

"…Hospice is a place where I feel safe. I can talk about what happened and not be afraid to share my feelings. Everyone there has been through a loss; I am not alone in my grief."

~ Richard Ballo, *Life without Lisa*

"Grief is itself a medicine..."
~ William Cowper, *Charity*

"We must embrace pain and burn
it as fuel for our journey."
~ Kenji Miyazawa

_____

_____

_____

_____

_____

_____

_____

_____

_____

_____

_____

_____

_____

_____

_____

_____

"If you're going through hell,
keep going."
~ Winston Churchill

"If you suppress grief too much, it can well redouble."

~ Molière

_____

_____

_____

_____

_____

_____

_____

_____

_____

_____

_____

_____

_____

_____

_____

_____

"Suppressed grief suffocates, it rages within
the breast, and is forced to multiply its strength."
~ Ovid

"The world is full of suffering, it is full
also of the overcoming of it."

~ Helen Keller

_____

_____

_____

_____

_____

_____

_____

_____

_____

_____

_____

_____

_____

_____

_____

_____

"...death is not the end. Our loved ones who have died are still very much around us."

~ Sandy Wiltshire, *My Gift of Light*

"When an emotional injury takes place, the body begins a process as natural as the healing of a physical wound. Let the process happen. Trust that nature will do the healing. Know that the pain will pass, and, when it passes, you will be stronger, happier, more sensitive and aware."

~ Dr. Melba Colgrove

_____

_____

_____

_____

_____

_____

_____

_____

_____

_____

_____

_____

_____

_____

"We are healed of a suffering
only by experiencing it to the full."
~ Marcel Proust

"Grief is a journey, often perilous and without clear direction, that must be taken. The experience of grieving cannot be ordered or categorized, hurried or controlled, pushed aside or ignored indefinitely. It is inevitable as breathing, as change, as love. It may be postponed, but it will not be denied."

~ Molly Fumia

_____

_____

_____

_____

_____

_____

_____

_____

_____

_____

_____

_____

_____

_____

_____

_____

"There are things that we don't want to happen but have to accept, things we don't want to know but have to learn, and people we can't live without but have to let go."
~ Author unknown

"There is no grief like
the grief that does not speak."

~ Henry Wadsworth Longfellow

_____

_____

_____

_____

_____

_____

_____

_____

_____

_____

_____

_____

_____

_____

_____

_____

_____

_____

_____

"What soap is for the body,
tears are for the soul."

~ Jewish Proverb

"Blessed are they that mourn,
for they shall be comforted."

~ The Holy Bible, Matthew 5:4

_____

_____

_____

_____

_____

_____

_____

_____

_____

_____

_____

_____

_____

_____

_____

_____

_____

_____

_____

"No one ever told me that
grief felt so like fear."
~ C.S. Lewis

"Oh that it were possible,
After long grief and pain,
To find the arms of my true love,
Around me once again."

~ Alfred Lord Tennyson

_____

_____

_____

_____

_____

_____

_____

_____

_____

_____

_____

_____

_____

"I never knew I had so many tears in me. I cried,
and sometimes I screamed. I journaled."
~ Diana Jacks, *Here to There, Grief to Peace*

"How dare the sun shine and the flowers bloom
and the garden be beautiful when my love is dead?"

~ Rebecca Rice

_____

_____

_____

_____

_____

_____

_____

_____

_____

_____

_____

_____

_____

_____

_____

_____

_____

"I receive mountains of mail with Lisa's name on it, yet I'm not ready to stop her mail. I would be telling the world she is dead and I am a widower."

~ Richard Ballo, *Life without Lisa*

"To everything there is a season,
and a time to every purpose under the heaven."

~ The Holy Bible, Ecclesiastes 3:1

_____

_____

_____

_____

_____

_____

_____

_____

_____

_____

_____

_____

_____

_____

_____

_____

"Everyone we have loved has become a part of us...
and no relationship, created in love, can ever die."
~ John E. Welshons, *Awakening from Grief*

"Never underestimate how angry you are! Grief and anger go together. As someone once said, 'Depression is merely anger without enthusiasm.' Anger is there for a reason. You must acknowledge it, even honor it, in order to dissipate it."

~ Diana Jacks, *Here to There, Grief to Peace*

_____

_____

_____

_____

_____

_____

_____

_____

_____

_____

_____

_____

_____

_____

"I am desperate to find someone to help me from sinking further into the abyss of grief, so I call Hospice….I visualize the grief counselors throwing each of us a rescue rope so we won't drown in our tears and fears."

~ Rich Ballo, *Life without Lisa*

"Your pain is the breaking of the shell
that encloses your understanding."
~ Kahlil Gibran

_____

_____

_____

_____

_____

_____

_____

_____

_____

_____

_____

_____

_____

"In my Lucia's absence
Life hangs upon me, and becomes a burden;
I am ten times undone, while hope, and fear,
And grief, and rage and love rise up at once,
And with variety of pain distract me."
~ Joseph Addison

"Near Death Experiencers return with a sense that everything in the universe is connected. An eloquent description of this feeling was given to me by a hard-driving, no-nonsense businessman who had an N.D.E. (Near Death Experience)... . One thing I learned when I died was that we are all part of one, big, living universe. We are connected with all things and if we send love along those connections, then we are happy."

~ Dr. Raymond Moody, M.D., Ph.D., *The Light Beyond*

_____

_____

_____

_____

_____

_____

_____

_____

_____

_____

_____

_____

_____

_____

_____

_____

"As a family, we found ways to talk about our sadness and express our feelings of loss. This helped me after my grandma...and my dad died."

~ Jenny Wheeler, *Weird Is Normal When Teenagers Grieve*

"It's so curious: one can resist
tears and 'behave' very well
in the hardest hours of grief.
But then someone makes you a
friendly sign behind a window,
or one notices that a flower that
was in bud only yesterday has
suddenly blossomed, or a letter
slips from a drawer...
and everything collapses."

~ Colette

"...I don't always feel ready to pick up the phone and talk to people...so I decide to write a letter based on some of my journal entries....I write that even though Lisa is dead, I will still be talking about her. I expect my friends to talk about her, too. They shouldn't be worried that mentioning her may cause me pain. I am already in pain, and if they choose to ignore Lisa, it will hurt me even more. It will be like a denial of her life and the life she, Victor, Nicholas and I had together."

~ Richard Ballo, *Life without Lisa*

"You need to face the pain and the fear
and walk through the grief."
~ Dr. Phil McGraw

"The deep pain that is felt at the death of every friendly soul arises from the feeling that there is in every individual something which is inexpressible, peculiar to him alone, and is, therefore, absolutely and irretrievably lost."
~ Arthur Schopenhauer

"Deep sobs -
That start beneath my heart
and hold my body in a grip that hurts.
The lump that swells inside my throat
brings pain that tries to choke.
Then tears course down my cheeks -
I drop my head in my so empty hands
abandoning myself to deep dark grief
and know that with the passing time
will come relief.
That though the pain may stay
There soon will come a day
When I can say her name
and be at peace."

~ Norah Leney

_____

_____

_____

_____

_____

_____

_____

_____

_____

_____

_____

_____

_____

_____

_____

"I do not believe that sheer suffering teaches.
If suffering alone taught, all the world would
be wise, since everyone suffers. To suffering
must be added mourning, understanding,
patience, love, openness, and the willingness
to remain vulnerable."

~ Anne Morrow Lindbergh

"I knew that…the full acceptance of the finality of loss, and all the pain that goes with it, need not diminish life but could give it a new quality of fulfillment. I also knew that this could not be achieved without going through the agonies of grief and mourning."

~ Lily Pincus

_____

_____

_____

_____

_____

_____

_____

_____

_____

_____

_____

_____

_____

_____

_____

_____

"An un-grieved loss remains forever alive in our
unconscious, which has no sense of time."
~ B.G. Simos

"The sorrow which has no vent in tears
may make other organs weep."
~ Dr. Francis Braceland

_____

_____

_____

_____

_____

_____

_____

_____

_____

_____

_____

_____

_____

_____

_____

_____

"Every evening I turn my worries over to God.
He's going to be up all night anyway."
~ Mary C. Crowley

"Tearless grief bleeds inwardly."
~ Christian Nevell Bovee

_____

_____

_____

_____

_____

_____

_____

_____

_____

_____

_____

_____

_____

_____

_____

_____

_____

_____

_____

_____

_____

_____

_____

_____

_____

_____

_____

_____

_____

_____

_____

_____

_____

_____

"Tears are the silent language of grief."

~ Voltaire

"He that conceals his grief finds no remedy for it."
~ Turkish Proverb

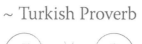

_____

_____

_____

_____

_____

_____

_____

_____

_____

_____

_____

_____

_____

_____

_____

_____

_____

_____

_____

_____

_____

_____

_____

_____

_____

_____

_____

"There is a sacredness in tears. They are not the mark of weakness, but of power. They speak more eloquently than ten thousand tongues. They are the messengers of overwhelming grief, of deep contrition, and of unspeakable love."

~ Washington Irving

"Sometimes, when only one person is missing,
the whole world seems depopulated."
~ Alphonse de Lamartine

"I see myself going through phases. I don't like the one I'm in now because I'm angry at Lisa for leaving me and abandoning our precious young sons. This is the cruelest irony of bereavement: the person I depend upon to help me in the tough times is not here in the most challenging moments of my life."

~ Richard Ballo, *Life without Lisa*

"Challenges are gifts that force us to search for a new center of gravity. Don't fight them. Just find a different way to stand."

~ Oprah Winfrey

_____

_____

_____

_____

_____

_____

_____

_____

_____

_____

_____

_____

_____

_____

_____

_____

_____

_____

"Gems may be precious
but friends are priceless."
~ Author unknown

"One doesn't discover new lands without consenting
to lose sight of shore for a very long time."
~ André Gide

_____

_____

_____

_____

_____

_____

_____

_____

_____

_____

_____

_____

_____

_____

_____

_____

_____

_____

_____

_____

_____

_____

_____

_____

_____

_____

_____

_____

_____

_____

_____

_____

_____

_____

_____

"Here is a test to find whether your mission
on earth is finished: if you're alive, it isn't."
~ Richard Bach, *Illusions*

"He who laughs, lasts."
~ Mary Pettibone Poole

_____

_____

_____

_____

_____

_____

_____

_____

_____

_____

_____

_____

_____

_____

_____

_____

"What is important…is to be honest and gentle
with yourself and to grieve in your own way… .
Your way of grieving may look odd to the
outside world, but that's okay."

~ Diana Jacks, *Here to There, Grief to Peace*

"Darkness cannot drive out darkness;
only light can do that."
~ Dr. Martin Luther King, Jr.

"I get by with a little help
from my friends."
~ John Lennon and Paul McCartney

"…I believe I shall in some
shape or other always exist… ."
~ Benjamin Franklin

"I know I am deathless..."

~ Walt Whitman, *Leaves of Grass*

"Piece by piece, I reenter the world. A new phase, a new body, a new voice. Birds console me by flying, trees by growing, dogs by the warm patch they leave on the sofa. Unknown people merely by performing their motions. It's like a slow recovery from a sickness, this recovery of one's self."

~ Tony Talbot

_____

_____

_____

_____

_____

_____

_____

_____

_____

_____

_____

_____

"...death is a passage into another place, (and) even though the events leading up to death can be agonizing, once a person gets out of his body there is no pain and, in fact, a great sense of relief...based on many N.D.E.s (Near Death Experiences), there will be a reunion with loved ones in the spiritual realm. That alone soothes many people (who are grief stricken)."

~ Dr. Raymond Moody, M.D., Ph.D., *The Light Beyond*

"When a man suffers, he ought not to say,
'That's bad!' Nothing that God imposes on man
is bad. But it is all right to say, 'That's bitter!'"
~ Hasidic saying

_____

_____

_____

_____

_____

_____

_____

_____

_____

_____

_____

_____

_____

_____

_____

_____

_____

_____

"…life entails a series of losses, we must learn to
use these losses creatively, not only to cope, but
to transcend and, beyond that, to grow."
~ Pesach Krauss, _Why Me? Coping with Grief, Loss and Change_

"All of mankind is of one Author...when one man dies,
one chapter is not torn out of the book, but translated
into a better language..."

~ John Donne

_____

_____

_____

_____

_____

_____

_____

_____

_____

_____

_____

_____

_____

_____

_____

_____

"When you are sorrowful look again in your heart,
and you shall see that in truth you are weeping for
that which has been your delight."
~ Kahlil Gibran

"I could remain in my grief, hurting both my family and myself, or I could cope with my grief in a healthier way. Expressing my feelings on paper even if only for myself, helped me to clarify things in my own head. It became a technique that I would use often and benefit from."

~ Sandy Wiltshire, *My Gift of Light*

_____

_____

_____

_____

_____

_____

_____

_____

_____

_____

_____

_____

_____

_____

_____

_____

"Time is a physician
that heals every grief."
~ Diphilus

"A man's dying is more the survivors' affair than his own."
~ Thomas Mann, *The Magic Mountain*

_____

_____

_____

_____

_____

_____

_____

_____

_____

_____

_____

_____

_____

_____

_____

_____

_____

"To spare oneself from grief at all cost can be
achieved only at the price of total detachment, which
excludes the ability to experience happiness."

~ Erich Fromm

"Everybody cries and
everybody hurts sometimes."

~ R.E.M.

"Pain is only bearable if we know
it will end, not if we deny it exists."
~ Viktor Frankl

"The most difficult thing of all—yet the most essential—is to love life, even when you suffer, because life is all."

~ Leo Tolstoy

_____

_____

_____

_____

_____

_____

_____

_____

_____

_____

_____

_____

_____

_____

_____

_____

_____

_____

"The path to healing from a loss is different for each person, one which may have many unexpected twists and turns, but a road that has been traveled by many."

~ Kirsti A. Dyer, M.D., M.S.

> "If you bring forth what is within you,
> what you bring forth will save you.
> If you do not bring forth what is within you,
> what you do not bring forth will destroy you."
>
> ~ Gnostic Scripture, Gospel of Thomas

_____

_____

_____

_____

_____

_____

_____

_____

_____

_____

_____

_____

_____

_____

_____

_____

_____

_____

"What happens (to the person who died) after death is so unspeakably glorious that our imagination and our feelings do not suffice to form even an approximate conception of it... ."

~ Carl Jung

"He'd begun to wake up in the morning with something besides dread in his heart. Not exactly happiness, not eagerness for a new day, but a kind of urge to be eager, a longing to be happy."

~ Jon Hasser

_____

_____

_____

_____

_____

_____

_____

_____

_____

_____

_____

_____

_____

_____

_____

_____

_____

_____

_____

_____

_____

_____

_____

_____

_____

_____

_____

_____

"Grief is a powerful, universal feeling,
but it is survivable."

~ Kirsti A. Dyer, M.D., M.S., *Living with Grief*

"And God shall wipe away all tears from their eyes, and there shall be no more death, neither sorrow, nor crying, neither shall there be any more pain; for the former things are passed away."

~ The Holy Bible, Revelation 21:4

"The words of the hospice grief counselor run through my brain. 'Grief is a process, not an event.'"
~ Richard Ballo, *Life without Lisa*

"Close your eyes and feel.
Breathe in the White Divine Love
God is sending you through…
angels from God."

~ Sandy Wiltshire, *My Gift of Light*

_____

_____

_____

_____

_____

_____

_____

_____

_____

_____

_____

_____

_____

_____

_____

_____

_____

_____

"…grief doesn't follow a precise linear path.…
Recovery from grief follows more of a zig-zag
line which…will slowly keep ascending."
~ Diana Jacks, *Here to There, Grief to Peace*

"One of the new emotions to surface was anger toward
Kim for leaving us. I was seeing a psychiatrist who provided
me a safe avenue to work through this feeling."
~ Sandy Wiltshire, *My Gift of Light*

_____

_____

_____

_____

_____

_____

_____

_____

_____

_____

_____

_____

_____

_____

_____

_____

_____

_____

_____

"Life is a great sunrise. I do not see why
death should not be an even greater one."
~ Vladimir Nabokov

"Rest assured that in her dying, in her flight through darkness toward a new light, she held you in her arms and carried your closeness with her. And when she arrived at God, your image was imprinted on her joy-filled soul."

~ Molly Fumia

_____

_____

_____

_____

_____

_____

_____

_____

_____

_____

_____

_____

_____

_____

_____

_____

_____

_____

_____

_____

_____

_____

_____

_____

_____

_____

_____

_____

"Everyone must row
with the oars he has."
~ English Proverb

"The best and most beautiful things in the world cannot be seen or even touched—they must be felt with the heart."

~ Helen Keller

_____

_____

_____

_____

_____

_____

_____

_____

_____

_____

_____

_____

_____

_____

"Sometimes when someone has
died we say, 'I feel like they're still here.'
That's because they are."

~ Marianne Williamson

"I enter the closet and hug her clothes. Her scent is here, her presence is here, and I want her to be in my arms again, but all I can hold are her clothes…Like an infant with its blankie, hugging (her) jersey to my chest comforts me."

~ Richard Ballo, *Life without Lisa*

_____

_____

_____

_____

_____

_____

_____

_____

_____

_____

_____

_____

_____

"Life can only be understood backwards;
but it must be lived forwards."
~ Søren Kierkegaard

"Sometimes a scream is better than a thesis."
~ Ralph Waldo Emerson

_____

_____

_____

_____

_____

_____

_____

_____

_____

_____

_____

_____

_____

_____

_____

_____

"Doing something your loved one loved to do
helps make 'first holidays' less painful."
~ Jenny Wheeler, *Weird Is Normal When Teenagers Grieve*

"All life is sacred. And since life is an affirmation of the Creator, I shall live on, even when I'm gone. In trailing clouds of glory shall I return to my Creator only to find that I had never even left. I shall walk among the lilies of the field and leave my trail in stardust in the sky."

~John Harricharan

_____

_____

_____

_____

_____

_____

_____

_____

_____

_____

_____

_____

_____

_____

"As I sat on her bed, I cried long and hard
for the daughter I lost. Wiping away the
tears, I knew I was ready to begin another
new chapter in my life."

~ Sandy Wiltshire, *My Gift of Light*

"Grieving takes us to the very heart of life itself.
Grieving takes us to love and to loss...
we all (are) going to die—which we can see as loss
of life or as a wave of transforming energy."
~ Deborah Morris Coryell,
Good Grief—Healing Through the Shadow of Loss

"...talk, cry, or scream if necessary....share and ventilate..."
~ Elisabeth Kübler-Ross, M.D., *On Death and Dying*

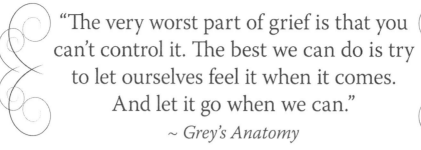

"The very worst part of grief is that you can't control it. The best we can do is try to let ourselves feel it when it comes. And let it go when we can."

~ *Grey's Anatomy*

_____

_____

_____

_____

_____

_____

_____

_____

_____

_____

_____

_____

_____

_____

_____

_____

_____

"There is a natural body, and there is a spiritual body...."

~ The Holy Bible, First Corinthians 15:35-52

"To find a safe journey through grief to growth does not mean one should forget the past. It means that on the journey we will need safe pathways so that remembrance, which may be painful, is possible."
~ Donna O'Toole, *Healing and Growing through Grief*

_____

_____

_____

_____

_____

_____

_____

_____

_____

_____

_____

_____

_____

_____

"When I come to the end of the road
And the sun has set for me
I want no rites in a gloom-filled room.
Why cry for a soul set free?

Miss me a little—but not too long
And not with your head bowed low.
Remember the love that we once shared,
Miss me—but let me go.

For this is a journey that we all must take,
And each must go alone.
It's all a part of the Master's plan,
A step on the road to home.

When you are lonely and sick of heart
Go to the friends we know.
And bury your sorrows in doing good deeds,
Miss me—but let me go!"

~ Anonymous, *Miss Me But Let Me Go*

"I have seen death too often to believe in death. It is not an ending–but a withdrawal. As one who finishes a long journey, stills the motor, turns off the lights, steps from his car, and walks up the path to the home that awaits him."

~ Don Blanding, *A Journey Ends*

_____

_____

_____

_____

_____

_____

_____

_____

_____

_____

_____

_____

_____

_____

_____

_____

"Before you can let in happy feelings, you must first let out the emotions that come with grief, just like you can't inhale a fresh breath until you exhale the old one."

~ Jenny Wheeler, *Weird Is Normal When Teenagers Grieve*

"I should get out more
I should not be so sad
I should talk about it
I should stop crying
I should hurt less
I should be better
I should be stronger
I should…stop 'shoulding' myself
I can cry when I need to
I can talk when I want to
I can be silent if it is right for me
I can hurt like I do
I can miss you forever
I can reinvest when I am ready
I can grieve how I want"

~ TheGriefToolBox.com

_____

_____

_____

_____

_____

_____

_____

"The soul always knows what to do to heal itself.
The challenge is to silence the mind."
~ Caroline Myss

"This grief, too, will not last. You may not believe it,
but it's true. Life will get better."

~ Diana Jacks, *Here to There, Grief to Peace*

_____

_____

_____

_____

_____

_____

_____

_____

_____

_____

_____

_____

_____

_____

_____

_____

"Things will never be exactly the same
after your loss, but that doesn't mean
you won't be happy again."
~ Jenny Wheeler,
Weird Is Normal When Teenagers Grieve

"You are forever altered when tragedy hits.
But you—wounded and scarred—have grown
in wisdom, compassion and strengths."

~ Diana Jacks, *Here to There, Grief to Peace*

_____

_____

_____

_____

_____

_____

_____

_____

_____

_____

"He has put on invisibility.
Dear Lord, I cannot see –
But this I know, although the road ascends
And passes from my sight,
That there will be no night;
That You will take him gently by the hand
And lead him on
Along the road of life that never ends,
And he will find it is not death but dawn.
I do not doubt that You are there as here,
And You will hold him dear."

~ James Dillet Freeman, *The Traveler*

"…it takes time to adjust, grow and heal…I wish the pain would end so I can move ahead. I know there are phases I must pass through…I realize, though, that this phase is preparing me for the next chapter in my life."

~ Richard Ballo, *Life without Lisa*

_____

_____

_____

_____

_____

_____

_____

_____

_____

_____

_____

_____

_____

_____

_____

_____

_____

_____

_____

_____

_____

_____

_____

_____

_____

_____

_____

_____

_____

_____

_____

"...a 'grief attack' is a time when an unexpected wave of grief comes crashing down upon us... (they) can be very unpredictable."
~ Jenny Wheeler, *Weird Is Normal When Teenagers Grieve*

"…we have found that those…do best who have been encouraged to express their rage, to cry… and to express their fears and fantasies to someone who can quietly sit and listen."

~ Elisabeth Kübler-Ross, M.D., *On Death and Dying*

_____

_____

_____

_____

_____

_____

_____

_____

_____

_____

_____

_____

_____

_____

_____

_____

"To have been loved so deeply, even though the person who loved us is gone, will give us some protection forever."

~ J.K. Rowling

"I take the small bottle of Chanel No. 5 perfume,
open it and inhale a flood of memories.
For an instant, I feel calm and loved."

~ Richard Ballo, *Life without Lisa*

Along the Road
"I walked a mile with Pleasure;
She chattered all the way.
But left me none the wiser
For all she had to say.
I walked a mile with Sorrow
And ne'er a word said she;
But oh, the things
I learned from her
When Sorrow
walked with me!"

~ Robert Browning Hamilton

"Do ordinary things with extraordinary love."
~ Mother Teresa

_____

_____

_____

_____

_____

_____

_____

_____

_____

_____

_____

_____

"According to the theory of aerodynamics,
the bumble bee is unable to fly. This is because
the size, weight and shape of its body in
relation to the total wing spread make flying
impossible. But the bumble bee, being ignorant
of these profound scientific truths, goes ahead
and flies anyway and manages to make a
little honey every day."

~ Author unknown

"Love cures people—both the ones who
give it and the ones who receive it."

~ Dr. Karl Menninger

"And remember, your loved ones are always with you, eternally alive in the warm, soft womb of your heart. You are not alone."
~ John E. Welshons, *Awakening from Grief*

"...you have the freedom to be yourself,
your true self, here and now and nothing
can stand in your way... ."
~ Richard Bach, *Jonathan Livingston Seagull*

_____

_____

_____

_____

_____

_____

_____

_____

_____

_____

_____

_____

_____

"Hope is our future.
It is our big chance."
~ Maurice Lamm, *The Power of Hope*

"Look forward and be hopeful, look backward
and be thankful, look downward and be
helpful, look upward and be humble."

~ Author unknown

_____

_____

_____

_____

_____

_____

_____

_____

_____

_____

_____

_____

_____

_____

"It is one of life's laws that as soon as
one door closes, another opens.
But the tragedy is we look at the closed
door and disregard the open one."
~ André Gide

"It is never too late to start living and growing."

~ Elisabeth Kübler-Ross, M.D., *Death: The Final Stage of Growth*

_____

_____

_____

_____

_____

_____

_____

_____

_____

_____

_____

_____

_____

_____

_____

_____

_____

_____

"Death is a natural part
of the web of life."
~ Barbara Harris Whitfield, *Final Passage*

"You can clutch the past so tightly to your chest that
it leaves your arms too full to embrace the present."

~ Jan Glidewell

_____

_____

_____

_____

_____

_____

_____

_____

_____

_____

_____

_____

_____

_____

_____

_____

"A grief attack is when I hold my breath
until it passes and then I can breathe again."
~ Richard Ballo, *Life without Lisa*

"Often just when you are thinking, 'Hey, I am handling this pretty well,' a flood of grief suddenly engulfs you. Any kind of reminder can be the catalyst...do not be surprised by being blind-sided."

~ Diana Jacks, *Here to There, Grief to Peace*

_____

_____

_____

_____

_____

_____

_____

_____

_____

_____

_____

_____

_____

_____

_____

_____

"Loss is nothing else but change,
and change is Nature's delight."
~ Marcus Aurelius

"I learned at Hospice…(about) a 'grief attack,' an acute upsurge of grief that can occur without warning. It can come out of the blue…I feel like I'm walking through an emotional mine field."

~ Richard Ballo, *Life without Lisa*

_____

_____

_____

_____

_____

_____

_____

_____

_____

_____

_____

_____

_____

_____

_____

_____

_____

_____

_____

"As long as I can I will look at this world for both of us. As long as I can I will laugh with the birds, I will sing with the flowers, I will pray to the stars, for both of us."

~ Posted on motivateus.com, Sascha

"Morning has broken,
Like the first morning,
Blackbird has spoken
Like the first bird;
Praise for the singing,
Praise for the morning,
Praise for them springing
Fresh from the Word."

~ Morning Has Broken,
Christian hymn,
Lyrics by Eleanor Farjeon

"Even the darkest night will
end and the sun will rise."
~ Victor Hugo, *Les Misérables*

"I believe that...hope always triumphs
over experience. That laughter is the cure for
grief...love is stronger than death."
~ Robert Fulghum

_____

_____

_____

_____

_____

_____

_____

_____

_____

_____

_____

_____

"One joy scatters
a hundred griefs."
~ Chinese Proverb

"Friendship doubles our joy
and divides our grief."

~ Swedish Proverb

"Time heals griefs and quarrels, for we change
and are no longer the same persons."
~ Blaise Pascal

"She was no longer wrestling with the grief,
but could sit down with it as a lasting companion
and make it a sharer in her thoughts."

~ George Eliot

"Joy comes, grief goes,
we know not how."
~ James Russell Lowell

"Suffering is not an elective, it is a core course in the University of Life."

~ Steven J. Lawson

_____

_____

_____

_____

_____

_____

_____

_____

_____

_____

_____

_____

_____

_____

_____

_____

_____

_____

"I still miss those I loved who are no longer with me but I find I am grateful for having loved them. The gratitude has finally conquered the loss."

~ Rita Mae Brown

"I have come to believe that caring for myself is not self-indulgent. Caring for myself is an act of survival."

~ Audre Lorde

_____

_____

_____

_____

_____

_____

_____

_____

_____

_____

_____

_____

_____

_____

_____

_____

"Grief has a quality of healing in it that is very deep
because we are forced to a depth of emotion that is
usually below the threshold of our awareness."

~ Steven Levine

"When it seems that our sorrow is too great to be borne,
let us think of the great family of the heavy-hearted
into which our grief has given us entrance, and inevitably,
we will feel about us, their arms and their understanding."

~ Helen Keller

"What you are now is what you have been,
what you will be is what you do now."
~ Buddha

"I find an old photograph
and see your smile.
As I feel your presence anew,
I am filled with warmth
and my heart...remembers love...."
~ *In Memory of You*

_____

_____

_____

_____

_____

_____

_____

_____

_____

_____

_____

_____

_____

_____

_____

_____

"We must accept finite
disappointment, but never
lose infinite hope."
~ Dr. Martin Luther King, Jr.

"If you learn from your suffering, and really come
to understand the lesson you were taught, you
might be able to help someone else who's
now in the phase you may have just completed.
Maybe that's what it's all about after all... ."

~ Author unknown

_____

_____

_____

_____

_____

_____

_____

_____

_____

_____

_____

_____

_____

"I have learned to forgive myself for feeling
angry at Lisa for dying; that's a normal reaction,
grief counselors have told me…I have learned
to let go of the guilt I carried for so long,
beating myself up because I thought there was
something else I could have done to save her."
~ Richard Ballo, *Life without Lisa*

"It is foolish and wrong to mourn
the men who died. Rather we should
thank God that such men lived."

~ George S. Patton, Jr.

_____

_____

_____

_____

_____

_____

_____

_____

_____

_____

_____

_____

_____

_____

"There are only two ways to live your life. One
is as though nothing is a miracle.
The other is as though everything is a miracle."
~ Albert Einstein

"Those who wish to sing
always find a song."

~ Plato

"And life is what we make it,
always has been, always will be."
~ Grandma Moses

"People in mourning have to come to grips with death before they can live again. Mourning can go on for years and years. It doesn't end after a year, that's a false fantasy. It usually ends when people realize that they can live again, that they can concentrate their energies on their lives as a whole, and not on their hurt, and guilt and pain."

~ Elisabeth Kübler-Ross. M.D.

_____

_____

_____

_____

_____

_____

_____

_____

_____

_____

_____

_____

_____

_____

_____

_____

_____

"Embrace your grief.
For there, your soul will grow."
~ Carl Jung

"Perhaps, they are not stars in the sky,
but rather openings where our loved ones
shine down to let us know they are happy."
~ Eskimo legend

_____

_____

_____

_____

_____

_____

_____

_____

_____

_____

_____

"You know nothing of yourself here and in this state.

You are like the wax in the honeycomb:
What does it know of fire or gutting?
When it gets to the stage of the waxen
Candle and when light is emitted, then it knows.

Similarly, you will know that
when you were alive you were dead,
And only thought yourself alive."

~ Idries Shah, *The Way of the Sufi*

Student questioning the master: "Master, how can I become a butterfly?" And the master responds: "You must want to change so much that you are willing to give up being a caterpillar."

~ Author unknown

_____

_____

_____

_____

_____

_____

_____

_____

_____

_____

_____

_____

_____

_____

"We fight to hold on to recent memories
even as, with a force like gravity, time
pulls us away from those who have died."
~ Michael Dorris

"It's only when we truly know and understand that we
have a limited time on earth—and that we have no way
of knowing when our time is up—that we will begin to live
each day to the fullest, as if it was the only one we had."
~ Elisabeth Kübler-Ross, M.D.

"Only he who suffers can be the
guide and healer of the suffering."
~ Thomas Mann

"I know for certain that we never
lose the people we love, even to death.
They continue to participate
in every act, thought and decision
we make. Their love leaves an
indelible imprint in our memories.
We find comfort in knowing that
our lives have been enriched by
having shared their love."

~ Leo Buscaglia

_____

_____

_____

_____

_____

_____

_____

_____

_____

_____

_____

_____

_____

"I have come a long way…I am proud of where
I was in my journey through grief and how far I
have come in assimilating her death into my life
and making a new life. I know grief will still visit
me from time to time, but I am alive, opening my
heart, and life is good. I have emerged as a stronger
person with a passion for living."

~ Richard Ballo, *Life without Lisa*

"If there ever comes a day when we can't be together,
keep me in your heart, I'll stay there forever."
~ Winnie the Pooh

_____

_____

_____

_____

_____

_____

_____

_____

_____

_____

_____

_____

_____

_____

"Grief can be brought on by pieces
of a song, old homes or places
we have been. The memories of
our life, once traumatic to think
about, are now pleasant thoughts
and I can smile at the memories."

~ Richard Ballo, *Life without Lisa*

"An important way to cope with grief is having an outlet,
be it interpersonal, be it artistic, that will allow you to not
have to contain your grief, but will give you an opportunity
to express it, to externalize it to some degree."

~ R. Benyamin Cirlin, Grief counselor

_____

_____

_____

_____

_____

_____

_____

_____

_____

_____

_____

_____

_____

"Tears have a wisdom all their own.
They come when a person has relaxed
enough to let go and to work through his
sorrow. They are the natural bleeding of an
emotional wound, carrying the poison out of
the system. Here lies the road to recovery."
~ F. Alexander Magoun

"Man can learn nothing except by
going from the known to the unknown."
~ Claude Bernard

"A cloud does not know why it moves in just such a direction and at such a speed. It feels an impulsion…this is the place to go now. But the sky knows the reasons and the patterns behind all clouds, and you will know, too, when you lift yourself high enough to see beyond horizons."

~ Richard Bach, *Illusions*

_____

_____

_____

_____

_____

_____

_____

_____

_____

_____

_____

_____

_____

_____

"Do all the good you can…
In all the ways you can
In all the places you can…
To all the people you can
As long as ever you can."
~ Unknown

"You can shed tears that she is gone,
or you can smile because she has lived.
You can close your eyes and pray that she will come back,
or you can open your eyes and see all she's left.
Your heart can be empty because you can't see her,
or you can be full of the love you shared.
You can turn your back on tomorrow and live yesterday,
or you can be happy for tomorrow because of yesterday.
You can remember her and only that she is gone,
or you can cherish her memory and let it live on.
You can cry and close your mind,
be empty and turn your back.
Or you can do what she'd want:
smile, open your eyes, love and go on."

~ David Harkins

> **Why is it difficult to talk about the end of our lives or the lives of our friends and loved ones? Why do we avoid the topic of death at all cost? Death is as much a part of life as birth. The more we talk about it and explore various beliefs, the more we demystify it and remove the "too terrible to talk about" voodoo curse of it. Then we are free to relax and accept it.**

The Universal Reality of Death, Dying and Its Impact

RELIGION AND POLITICS are two subjects regarded as most abhorred in polite company, but there's one that's even more verboten: death and dying.

How peculiar is that since not one of us is getting out of here alive? But the truth is, our mortality terrifies us. Granted, there is a community that deals with death and dying which includes lawyers, doctors, nurses, counselors and therapists. They work crafting wills and trusts. They prepare bodies for funeral viewing. Counselors, therapists and grief support groups offered by Hospice, churches, and mental health associations are widely available. Yet conversation with our friends rarely touch on the subject.

The words we use to describe the person who died sometimes depends upon our closeness to the deceased, the length of time since they died and the degree of our willingness to be vulnerable. We use terms to describe what happened such as our loved one is deceased, lost, late, has passed on, made their transition, is dead, died, or departed. The deceased often leaves behind a spouse or significant other, children, siblings, cousins, friends and sometimes parents, and even grandparents. Often the wake the departed leave behind is wide which means the number of people profoundly impacted is great.

Each death has widespread impact

One death affects a web of relationships from family and friends to community members, neighbors, business associates, church congregants and their families. Over 6,700 people die each day in the United States. Factor in their family members, friends and business colleagues to see the exponential impact each death has. Usually thousands of people are touched by each death–yet so few want to talk of death and dying.

Why is it difficult talking about the end of our lives? Why is it difficult to talk to an attorney about what to do with our accumulated stuff after we die? Why does it make us gulp when confronted by making out a living will prior to surgery just because we want to be prepared? Perhaps we fear death because we have no control over how or when we die, and to imagine ourselves as not being alive on earth is unthinkable. Just as birth brings us into the world of light and air, death takes us away into a whole new level of light. Where we were before birth and where we go after death sparks much debate and the answer we give to those questions depends on personal and religious beliefs.

Grieving is a process

Widowers, widows and parents know all too well the disbelief of the reality of death, the guilt, depression, and despair that often overwhelm those left behind. Grief can be ignored for a while, but it doesn't go away until we face it, accept it, and deal with it. We must go through a process to once again know laughter, joy, happiness, and the bitter-sweet satisfaction of recovery from grief and to fully live again.

Recognizing your deep feelings and allowing the grief to be expressed will make all the difference. Share with a trusted friend and keep a journal of your thoughts and feelings. Seek help from a professional—you could benefit from someone else's wise counsel and support after you've suffered unthinkable loss. Grab onto a lifeline, seek professional help from a therapist or counselor who is a death and dying expert. Often Hospices offer qualified, thoughtful, loving and exceedingly helpful professionals with whom you can meet either in a one-on-one private counseling setting or grief recovery group setting.

Give grief its due

Being able to talk and write about what you are going through and how you feel will make all the difference in the world. Expressing your pain, your regrets, and your aching loss is the path to healing without question. Yes, it seems impossible that you will ever smile again, enjoy life and wake up with a light heart. The sooner you give grief its due, the sooner you will have a life worth living again.

Shakespeare knew the route to healing grief:

> "Give sorrow words. The grief that does not speak whispers the o'erfraught heart and bids it break."
> ~ William Shakespeare, *Macbeth*

Even though it seems impossible to believe, expressing grief will bring acceptance, healing and eventually a happy life again. Trust the process, trust the outcome.

How to reduce stress and trauma when a loved one dies is important and challenging at the same time. I turned to journaling to help recover after my wife Lisa died. Since then I have spoken across the country on the topic of grief and healing after loss. In this article, I include my tried and true approaches and tips to reduce suffering and bring the surviving person back into life.

Seven Ways to Cope with the Death of a Loved One

COUNTLESS STUDIES HAVE PROVEN that stress causes illness, disease and even death, yet life is often filled with stress. So when stress overwhelms you, is serious disease in your future? Or is there a way to avoid illness, reduce the stress and get back to living a fulfilling life?

Of course, some stresses take a bigger toll than others. Certainly, losing a job is a high level stress; divorce is another. But perhaps the ultimate stress one can suffer is the death of a loved one. Is a serious health threat inevitable for you when someone you love dies? Could be, unless you take action.

According to the *British Medical Journal,* chronic job stress leads to heart disease and diabetes. It's also been proven that the loss of a spouse can be fatal for the spouse left behind. In fact, one study discovered that people rate the death of a spouse as the number one stress of a lifetime. *The New England Journal of Medicine* revealed that the death rate of a spouse accelerated after their other half was merely hospitalized. The risk of death associated with a spouse's hospitalization is higher for men (22%) than women (16%). Not surprisingly, the year following the death of a spouse, the death rate of the surviving spouse spikes significantly. Yet it need not be that way.

Getting out of bed was a loathsome thought

I am no stranger to the stress suffered when a spouse dies. When my beloved wife succumbed to cancer, it took the full force of my will merely to get out of bed in the morning. I admit I might have just stayed in bed and "waited for the inevitable," if it weren't for my five and six year old boys who needed me more than ever.

After the excruciating loss of my wife to cancer, my life's purpose became muddled; I no longer found joy or fulfillment in life. My emotional state took me on a constant roller coaster ride. Not only was I suddenly thrown into the unthinkable void associated with the death of my adored life partner, but I wrestled with the death of my dreams as well.

Zombie-like, I went through the motions, but my heart was crushed and life had lost its joy. Following the dictates of society that men should not show emotion, I wept in private. But soon the urge to write down my thoughts and feelings took over and became a pivotal factor to save me. I silently turned to my notepad for comfort. Every day I committed my emotions and experiences to paper as I navigated a new life course. Journaling gave me a safe place to express the un-expressible and to vent my feelings. Without this outlet, the toll on my health would have been catastrophic.

My grief journal turned into an award-winning book

Little did I know that years later my grief journal would become the award winning book–*Life without Lisa–A Widowed Father's Compelling Journey Through the Rough Seas of Grief*–a book whose intent is to help others through the loss of a loved one.

A decade after Lisa's death, I started to speak to people across the country, sharing my personal story, lending an empathetic ear and offering what most helped me pull out of the deepest, darkest hole and return to a meaningful life. I continue to speak to this day.

Without question, journaling was the number one therapy I used to regain my emotional and mental health. Little by little, my own written words charted my healing process. In addition, the boys and I took advantage of bereavement counseling offered by our local Hospice: Avow in Naples, Florida. There I found a support system to bolster my shattered emotions, guidance to assist in my decision making and programs to help my suffering sons.

What helped me most to recover

When all was said and done, I gained help from a number of sources and activities. Here are my top seven tips to return to health and happiness after losing a loved one:

1. Journal your feelings without holding back–allow yourself to vent every thought, feeling and emotion, regardless of how "good or bad" they seem to you.

2. Enlist support and help from your local hospice or bereavement group.

3. Give yourself permission to take "as long as it takes" to recover.

4. When able, do something for someone else. Volunteer to help others.

5. Take care of yourself by doing things that make you feel better: get regular massages, take long walks, listen to music, or sleep late.

6. Do something different at holiday time; find new ways to celebrate, establish new traditions.

7. Talk about your loved one to friends and family; encourage them to speak your loved one's name and share their favorite reminiscences with you.

I believe because I took these steps to help myself through these darkest of times, I was able to avoid severe health challenges. Today I am well and happy. I sit on the Hospice board of directors at Avow of Naples, I am a member and served as president of my local Kiwanis club, I have funded two scholarships: one at my alma mater, Suffolk University, and one in Lisa's memory at Florida Gulf Coast University. These are some of the ways of giving back to the community and to the future community.

My boys have grown into strong, well-balanced, happy young men. Once again, my life is full, meaningful and happy. Despite the fact that I didn't think that could ever be possible, the steps I took to help myself paid off in the most meaningful of ways.

I encourage anyone suffering from grief to keep a journal. It helped me pull through and return to a happy life. I highly recommend it.

Mother's Day and Father's Day can be extremely challenging for children who have lost a parent as well as for parents who have lost a child. These days of celebration have such impact that often even people in their sixties still lament the loss of one or both parents. Imagine how difficult this can be for children!

I discovered there are ways to make Mother's or Father's Day more tolerable for your children after your spouse has died. In my case, my wife had died, but the suggestions I offer here regarding Mother's Day are applicable to Father's day as well.

Through trial and error, I discovered there are ways to help your children heal after their staggering loss. Here's what helped my children the most and ideas that have the potential to help you, too.

How to Handle Mother's or Father's Day if Your Spouse Has Passed Away

MOTHER'S DAY OBVIOUSLY BRINGS to mind all things maternal–warm and wonderful hugs, children's homemade cards, a delicious dinner, and mom's loving smile and kisses. As Mother's Day arrived each year for more than a decade after my wife died, I knew my now-grown children would obviously have to celebrate the day in ways far different from other children. Together we figured out the approaches that worked best for the boys, but it took some thinking and doing.

Although my wife was battling cancer, we were still an intact family living life the best we could. But despite Lisa's relentless fight, she lost that battle at age 38 leaving me to raise our five and six year old sons.

She passed away just before Christmas and five months later I was facing Mother's Day without the boys' mother. Without question, this poignant reminder brought more grief into our lives. I tried to focus on ways to make that day and experience less traumatizing for my kids.

I gave a lot of thought to what would help Victor and Nick get through Mother's Day in the best, least painful way possible. We evolved the process over the years and now I can recommend the following five approaches to help you and your kids celebrate Mother's Day or Father's Day if they don't have a mother or father present in their lives.

1. Remember the good times. Pictures are great for triggering memories. Bring them out and talk to your kids about the day each picture was taken. Share the life you and your wife or husband were dreaming about and how you felt about having kids. Keep the talk on an age appropriate level. There will be days to come when they are older and can understand more. Always reassure them that you and they are a team and you have no intention of leaving them.

2. Establish new routines. A new routine can be simple or elaborate. One of the first Mother's Day after my wife died, I bought roses. The kids and I went to the local pier and threw the roses into the Gulf of Mexico. Yes, we looked out of place in our Sunday best among the swimsuit set, but we were on a mission. The boys enjoyed participating in this unique tribute to their beloved mother.

3. Find a "new mom or dad" for the children to honor. This doesn't mean getting married so your children have a stepmother or father in their lives. It means find a mom or dad substitute–a sister/brother, aunt/uncle, grandmother/grand father, or special female/male friend to whom your young children can send cards and write messages to. This helps remove the stigma of being a motherless or fatherless child in elementary school. My boys chose their aunt Stephanie and my mother.

4. Encourage your kids to write a letter to their mom or dad. When having kids write such a letter, make sure they know it is for them and their mom or dad only and that no one else will read it. You might want to put the letters into an envelope for safekeeping. If the kids are open to it, you can read last year's letter before writing a new one. You can save their letters and eventually when the kids are older and get married, you can return them to them.

5. Eat cake. Go to a movie or rent a movie. Kids don't want to sit and grieve. They don't want to sit period. Get up and get out of the house. Shoot basketballs, throw a baseball, play miniature golf or go to a zoo. Enjoy a new day.

Remind them that even if their mother or father isn't physically around, they still have a mother/father who loves them dearly. If your children are in elementary school, remember there often is a Mother's Day and Father's Day card making activity at school and conversations about moms and dads. It can be a hard time for them. Discuss ahead of time who they will make cards for.

Being a parent is difficult and challenging. Being a single parent with young kids is hard. Help your kids make it through Mother's Day or Father's Day by trying new approaches to a tough situation. Both my sons and I not only survived but thrived. I assure you that you and your children can do it too.

Is it possible to survive Valentine's Day if you don't have a Valentine? How in the world can you get through February 14th if your beloved has died? At first I just wanted to pull the covers over my head and stay in bed, but since then I have developed five ways people can successfully get through Valentine's Day without their Valentine.

Five Ways to Feel Good on February 14th Even if Your Loved One Is Gone

VALENTINE'S DAY IS THE MOST two-some holiday of the entire year. But what if you have no Valentine, no significant other? What if your beloved Valentine has died and yet you are besieged with cupids, hearts and images of love, love, love as Valentine's Day approaches? I know this heartbreak first hand and as a result, I have developed tips for those who are in the same boat.

After my dearly beloved wife, Lisa, died of cancer in her late thirties, every day was painful. Christmas, Thanksgiving, her birthday, and our anniversary were, of course, heartbreaking. But the worst was Valentine's Day–probably because it felt like the entire world was in love and had their loved one by their side–except for me, of course. So in order to ease my emotional pain, I found ways to feel better on Valentine's Day.

Here are the five tips I put together for getting through Valentine's Day without a Valentine. These tips have gelled from my personal research and experience. I hope your emotional pain of being alone on Valentine's Day can be eased by trying a few of my tips.

1. Make someone else's day enjoyable. Volunteer at a nursing home or Hospice and hand out valentines, bring cookies to share and make your entire focus about helping someone else feel better.

2. Get physical, call a friend or acquaintance who is also missing their true love and plan to do something fun together on Valentine's Day. Hint: ignore the romantic restaurant scene–go rock climbing, ride bicycles, go kayaking, work out or take a walk instead!

3. Bring flowers and candy to an elderly person in your neighborhood. Stay for an extended chat and give the gift of listening to your neighbor's stories about her or

his life—even if you've heard them many times. Remember your parents and your adult children on Valentine's Day. Tell them how much you love them and how grateful you are to have them in your life.

4. Throw a Valentine's Day party for little children—your own, your grandchildren, friends' and neighbors' children. Decorate a big box with red and white crêpe paper, cut a slot in the cardboard and have the children "mail" their valentines. You could have them make their own valentines at the party and then "mail them" in the decorated box. You can distribute the valentines after you serve cookies and ice cream.

5. Treat yourself with love and caring. Send yourself flowers. Watch your favorite movie. Treat yourself to a special bottle of wine and exquisite cheese. Indulge in a spa treatment—a massage, manicure, pedicure, or facial can help you feel good and more positive about yourself. Be your own valentine. This final "treat yourself" tip is perhaps the most important tip of all

Holiday time is often the most difficult time of all after suffering a death. Grief naturally follows the death of a loved one, but sometimes grief expands during the holidays. No one can bring your loved one back, but there are ways to approach Christmas, Hanukkah and New Year celebrations to minimize your sadness and bring you some measure of joy and happiness. Here are eight tips to help you through this challenging season.

Eight Ways to Get Through the Holidays after the Death of a Loved One

THE HOLIDAYS ARE NOT NECESSARILY a happy, merry time—especially for people whose loved one has died during the past year, or even the past several years. In fact, if you're one of multi-millions of people who suffer such a loss each year, the holidays tend to increase the feelings of grief and despair.

Over four million people die each year in the U.S. leaving countless loved ones engulfed in grief. If you're one of those grieving, chances are the holidays only accentuate your sadness and sense of loss.

Are there ways to get through Christmas, Hanukkah and the New Year with minimal suffering and some level of enjoyment? Please be assured there are ways to make the holidays more bearable and even pleasant.

I know this journey first hand. My wife Lisa died just 10 days before Christmas. It made the first holiday season without Lisa nearly unbearable. Although I spent that first Christmas like a zombie, in subsequent years I found ways that helped me and can help you have a far more positive experience. Here are my personal tips to get through the holidays after suffering the death of a loved one:

1. Turn to Hospice for help. Hospice is not only for the dying, but for the living as well. Hospice provides individual and group counseling for those left behind.

2. Keep your expectations for yourself and the holidays reasonable. Don't put undue pressure on yourself by "demanding" that you act and feel a certain way.

200

Things will be different and probably not as merry as before—at least for a while. But you can experience some degree of happiness and enjoyment.

3. Feel your feelings. Don't stuff them down. Cry and feel sad. But don't allow them to engulf you. Have a written list of things you can do that will help you feel better—watch a funny movie, listen to uplifting music, play your favorite sport, meditate, take a bubble bath, engage in your absolutely favorite hobby.

4. Do something for someone else. Serve Christmas dinner at a soup kitchen or sing carols in a nursing home. Get outside of yourself and your own miseries and bring joy to others. In turn, it will bring tremendous joy to you.

5. Surround yourself with supportive, loving people. If you're with your family, wrap yourself in their love and caring.

6. Give yourself a break. Don't feel like you have to make the holidays happen for others. Pass the baton to someone else without feeling any guilt. Let someone else cook the turkey and clean up the kitchen. Be a pampered person!

7. Reminisce with family and friends. Talk openly about your loved one and share memories with others. Let laughter and happy times remind you of your loved one's life.

8. Journal, journal, journal. Write out your feelings and thoughts; commit them to paper. It is a remarkably healing process—scientific research proves it. Journaling will help you get through the holidays and, if you continue to journal, it will take you well beyond.

Hospice Provides Invaluable Help for the Living as Well as for Those Dying

A SOCIAL WORKER at the Massachusetts hospital where my wife had worked as a nurse, the very same hospital where she died, advised that I join a hospice counseling group in order to help me cope with Lisa's death. The social worker pointed out that most likely Hospice would offer programs for not only me, but for my five and six year old sons as well. She was right, and it turned out to be some of the best advice I ever received.

My wife, Lisa, and I were finishing a move from Massachusetts to Naples, Florida. We had already bought a house and furnished it. Our business opened in Naples. On a trip to a wedding up north Lisa's health deteriorated dramatically, and she entered the hospital. Two months later she died, and I was beyond bereft. The depth of my grief and loss defies words. Walking from one room to the other in our old home was a challenge, and I felt fortunate to put one foot in front of the other.

I decided the best thing to do was to go back to Naples to live. It felt hollow without her, to say the least, but I could not think past the idea of completing the plans we had already set in motion for our lives.

Thanks to the recommendation of the social worker, I contacted Avow Hospice in Naples two weeks after the boys and I arrived. I just knew I had to get help–I could barely function and think straight.

Hospice was a lifesaver

I joined a Hospice grief group and spent a year going to weekly meetings. At first, it was horribly painful. I was extremely uncomfortable. Often I would weep in the car after the meetings. I was an emotional mess because the group experience pretty much forced me to relive the horror of Lisa's death and face the fact that she was dead. When others shared their experiences, it just brought home how devastating the whole thing was to me.

I forced myself to continue because somewhere deep inside I knew this process was my lifeline. I simply had to keep going. The group experience was valuable on so many levels, but especially for showing me that the feelings I had and the experiences I was going

202

through were normal. I thought I had perhaps turned schizophrenic—one day I would feel some degree of happiness and the next I would crash and burn. I discovered through this hospice-for-the-living experience that having such grief attacks was completely normal. That helped me a great deal. In addition, I had a positive attitude: I knew Hospice could help me so I persevered.

At the same time, I enrolled our sons Victor and Nick in an Avow Hospice support group held at the local elementary school. The boys were relieved to discover they weren't the "only ones." Other kids had lost a parent and that awareness helped them realize they could talk with others who understood what they were going through.

A year later, I was ready to move on

After attending weekly Hospice grief group sessions for a year, I realized I was ready to fly out of the proverbial nest. I noticed when new people joined our group it made me aware of just how far I had come in the healing process. I knew it was time for me to assess if this was still helpful or had I grown beyond this phase. I decided I had thankfully grown beyond the stage the group focused on.

I still had a great deal of healing to achieve, but I had successfully graduated from the first stage. I was ready to seek out other modes of healing and help.

Lisa died in 1993, and I went to my first grief support group in 1994. The boys and I gained so much from Avow Hospice. My association with Avow Hospice has come full circle. Today I commit my time and resources to them. I sit on Avow Hospice's Board of Directors, their Physician's Advisory Board, and the Spiritual Advisory Board, as well as represent them in the community. I really don't know how I would have handled the turbulent years following my wife's death without Avow Hospice's assistance.

By hospice standards, Avow is considered to be a large hospice. They have 16 in-house beds and serve over 200 people each day mostly in their homes and retirement homes. The staff totals 150 of the most caring, compassionate people you can imagine. Avow is run by nurses—the CEO and CFO are both nurses and the staff is extremely loyal to the organization. Without question, patients come first.

Where to find help

The National Hospice and Palliative Care Organization offers a website filled with information and resources. The URL is http://www.nhpco.org/templates/1/homepage.cfm. You can check out the national organization as well as look under "Find a hospice or palliative care program" to discover a local program. If you need assistance, you can call the NHPCO helpline at 800-658-8898.

Whether you need their services for the dear one who is in the process of dying or for those left behind, Hospice will be there for you offering the best possible assistance. You can count on it just like I did.

Grief Resources

Quality of Life Publishing—Website: www.QoLPublishing.com

Quality of Life is an independent publishing house dedicated to educating physicians and communities served by hospice and home care agencies. They offer a wide range of end-of-life publications including heartfelt gentle grief support books and booklets. Since 1999, Quality of Life has published millions of newsletters, branded booklets, and grief support books, helping to ease the way for countless patients and families facing the end of life.

Booklets

When Death is Near
When You Are Grieving
When Teens Are Grieving
Grieving for Your Pet
Hospice Can Help
What is Palliative Care?
Caregiver Confidence

Books

Here to There, Grief to Peace
Afterglow
Life without Lisa
My Gift of Light
Weird Is Normal When Teenagers Grieve
Isabelle's Dream
Timmy's Christmas Surprise
Heart-Shaped Pickles
Penny Bear's Gift of Love
Reflections of a Loving Partner
Spiritual Care to Elderly and Dying Loved Ones
Real Men Do Cry
Tea with Elisabeth
Everyday Symbols for Joyful Living

Quality of Life Publishing
6210 Shirley Street, Suite 112
Naples, FL 34109
Toll-Free (U.S. and Canada): 877-513-0099
Phone: 239-513-9907
Fax: 239-513-0088
Email: info@qolpublishing.com

National Hospice & Palliative Care Organization (NHPCO)
Website: www.nhpco.org

1731 King Street, Suite 100
Alexandria, Virginia 22314
Phone: 703-837-1500
Fax: 703-837-1233 (fax)
Email: nhpco_info@nhpco.org

HelpLine: 800-658-8898–provides free consumer information regarding hospice care and puts the public in direct contact with hospice programs. Multilingual HelpLine: 877-658-8896–translated in over 200 languages.

Hospice Foundation of America–Website: www.hospicefoundation.org

1710 Rhode Island Ave, NW, Suite 400
Washington, DC 20036
Toll free: 800-854-3402
Phone: 202-457-5811

Young Widows and Widowers–Website: www.youngwidowsandwidowers.org

P.O. Box 5135
Andover, MA 01810-5135
Phone: 978-979-8993

The Compassionate Friends–Website: www.compassionatefriends.org

They assist families toward the positive resolution of grief following the death of a child of any age.

1000 Jorie Blvd.
Suite 140
Oak Brook, IL 60523
Toll-free: 877-969-0010, Fax: 630-990-0246
Email: nationaloffice@compassionatefriends.org

About Author Richard Ballo

RICHARD BALLO has been a professional writer since 1980 and earned his degree in journalism from Suffolk University in Boston in 1986. His first book, *Life without Lisa—A Widowed Father's Compelling Journey Through the Rough Seas of Grief* won the President's Award from the Florida Publishers' Association.

When Rich married his wife Lisa, he had a successful career as a technical writer. After their two sons were born, Rich left his position to become a stay-at-home dad and home-school teacher. He maintained his journalism prowess by writing freelance feature articles for the local newspaper in central Massachusetts.

After Lisa died at age 38, writer's block overwhelmed Rich and grief threatened to smother him in an avalanche of suffering. Little did he realize that the journal he had been keeping to record his thoughts, feelings and experiences in the aftermath of his wife's death would one day be published as an award-winning book that would serve as a beacon of hope for others charting their way through the black waters of grief.

Community involvement is a major focus for Rich today. He deeply believes in giving back to the community both financially as well as through personal service. He sits on the Board of Directors of Avow Hospice of Naples, FL, and is dedicated to supporting Hospice in a variety of ways including serving on Avow Hospice's Physicians' Advisory Board and their Spiritual Advisory Board as well. He speaks nationwide on the subject of healing grief after the loss of a loved one, promotes Hospice wherever he goes and frequently does Hospice fundraisers. He is a popular speaker and talk show guest.

His community service has also included serving on the Seacrest Country Day School's Board of Directors and being active in Kiwanis where he served as president. In addition, he has established and supports two scholarship funds, food banks, and The Salvation Army.

Rich, in addition to being the author of this *The Heart of Grief Relief Journal*, is currently working on several other books, both nonfiction and fiction. His sons Nick and Victor are in their 20's and thriving. Rich lives in Naples, Florida.

Rich may be contacted through his websites www.TheHeartofGriefRelief.com, www.RichardBallo.com or www.TolmanMainPress.com.

The Heart of Grief Relief Kit

Think of this as a first aid kit for your grieving heart. This unique bereavement kit contains a variety of things to aid you on your healing path until you finally do achieve relief from grief.

This kit was conceived by Rich Ballo who lost his 38-year-old wife Lisa when Rich was only a year older than she. Their sons were five and six years old. The loss was devastating for all.

Since nothing like *The Heart of Grief Relief Kit* existed, he obviously could not take advantage of it. But various components of the kit were available to him, and he used them to great advantage. He offers this assemblage to you to speed and ensure your own recovery.

Designed to help you:

- *Work through your grief.*
- *Find peace at the end of your healing from grief journey.*
- *Move beyond your loss.*
- *Embrace the pain in order to open your heart.*
- *Work through and banish feelings of helplessness, disorientation, utter despair and numbness.*
- *Get on with your life.*
- *Embrace the new, albeit different, life that lies before you.*

The Kit Components:

The Heart of Grief Relief Journal–a journal, a book, an inspiration, a resource guide all rolled into one. Journaling is an invaluable healing tool, and it was pivotal to Rich's recovery. Here is more than a journal–a balm for your soul.

Life without Lisa–This award-winning book candidly chronicles Rich Ballo's healing journey that spans the five years following his wife Lisa's death. Its pages reveal the depths of Rich's despair and his ultimate healing. It will reassure you that whatever you are feeling is normal and that the road to grief relief will take many twists and turns–but that you absolutely can get there from here.

Grief Relief Stress Heart–Keep this squeezable heart handy at your desk or wherever you most frequently are. The heart shape reminds you that the path to grief relief is through your heart. Squeezing this heart provides an escape valve for tensions you may feel.

Grief Relief Door Hanger–This handy alert can be kept on the doorknob to your office or bedroom–or whatever room you prefer. It acknowledges that some days will be better than others, and this can silently and effectively alert others whether or not it is a good day to enter or to let you suffer a grief attack in private. One side of the door hanger invites the visitor in. The other side may be displayed when you truly want to be alone. It warns that a grief attack is in process, please do not disturb.

Grief Relief Heart Key Ring–This key ring serves a dual purpose: to remind you that the path to grief relief truly does run through your heart and that you may be delighted at the benefits you receive when you jump in the car and drive to Hospice for group and/or private bereavement counseling.

Ball Point Journal Pen–This ball point *Heart of Grief Relief* pen may be used to write in your journal to express your deepest concerns and feelings.

When You Are Grieving Booklet–*When You Are Grieving* is an easy-to-read, gentle guide to healing for people who have suffered the death of a loved one. It not only reassures, soothes and guides adults struggling with grief, but also includes special tips for children and teens. It clearly explains the grieving process in an extremely helpful way. This booklet helps those left behind to better understand their grief, find comfort, and move forward with hope.

The Heart of Grief Relief Kit--$34.94

Each kit includes:

- *The Heart of Grief Relief Journal*
- *Life without Lisa*
- Grief Relief Squeezable Stress Heart
- Grief Relief Door Hanger
- Grief Relief Heart Key Ring
- Grief Relief Journal Pen
- *When You Are Grieving* booklet

(All kit components come packaged in a sturdy plastic bag with the Heart of Grief Relief logo on the front. Your own custom label can be added to the front of the bag.)

To order the journal and/or kit, please email Orders@Bookmasters.com, call 1-800-Booklog and/or go to www.AtlasBooks.com.

Questions regarding quantity discounts may be sent to RichardBallo@TheHeartofGriefRelief.com